Brain Bridges Cookbook

Hayley Venard

In collaboration with Dietitian Talha Ahmad

Dedication:

To all the passionate home cooks and culinary adventurers,

This cookbook is lovingly dedicated to you. Your unwavering commitment to the art of cooking, your relentless pursuit of flavors and textures, and your desire to create meals that nourish both the body and the soul inspire us every day.

Within these pages, we have gathered a collection of recipes that celebrate the joys of gastronomy and the power of food to bring people together, while including nutrition that boosts brain health.

Above all, this dedication is a tribute to the joy of sharing food with loved ones. May this cookbook inspire memorable gatherings and heartwarming conversations around the dining table. May it be a source of laughter, comfort, and connection, as we celebrate the simple pleasure of breaking bread together.

Thank you for embracing the culinary arts with passion and enthusiasm. Your dedication to the craft fuels our own, and it is our greatest pleasure to present this cookbook as a token of our gratitude and admiration.

Happy cooking!

Hayley Venard

CONTENTS

ACKNOWLEDGMENTS

Thank you so much to our dietitian, Talha Ahmad, for writing our recipes and providing detailed nutritional information!

1 BREAKFAST

Breakfast, the first meal of the day, holds a special place in our hearts and our routines. It awakens our senses and prepares us for the adventures that lie ahead. As the sun rises, we gather around the table, eager to indulge in the comforting rituals that accompany this morning feast.

The aroma of freshly brewed coffee fills the air, mingling with the tantalizing scents of sizzling bacon, buttery pancakes, and warm toast. It's a symphony of flavors, a symphony that fuels our bodies and nourishes our souls.

Breakfast offers us a moment of tranquility before the hustle and bustle of the day takes over. It's a time to gather with loved ones, sharing stories, laughter, and dreams over steaming mugs of tea or glasses of freshly squeezed orange juice. It's a reminder that amidst the chaos of life, there is always a place for connection and togetherness.

From simple bowls of cereal to elaborate spreads of eggs benedict and smoked salmon, breakfast offers endless possibilities. It caters to our cravings, providing the sustenance we need to conquer the challenges that await us. With each bite, we savor the flavors, the textures, and the nourishment that breakfast provides.

Beyond its physical benefits, breakfast symbolizes new beginnings. It signifies a fresh start, a chance to seize the day and make it our own. It infuses us with energy, motivation, and a sense of purpose. As we savor our morning meal, we awaken not only our taste buds but also our aspirations, setting the stage for a day filled with productivity and fulfillment.

So, let us raise our forks and toast to the beauty of breakfast. May it forever remain a cherished ritual, a time-honored tradition that nurtures our bodies, uplifts our spirits, and sets the tone for a day filled with endless possibilities.

Scrambled Eggs:

Serves: 1 ½

Ingredients

- 3 large eggs
- 1tsp. milk
- 1tsp. extra virgin olive oil
- Sea salt, black pepper
- Chopped chives (optional)

Instructions

- Heat pan on medium flame.
- Whisk eggs in a bowl, add 1tsp milk.
- Pour mixture on heated pan and scramble eggs on the pan.

BON APPETITE!

Scrambled Eggs

NUTRITION FACTS 1 ½ servings

Calories: 212kcals| Carbohydrates: 1.5g| Protein: 14.1g |
Fat: 16g | Saturated
Fat: 4.2g | Cholesterol: 470mg | Sodium: 155mg | Potassi
um: 170mg | Fiber: 0g

HEALTH BENEFITS: Eggs contain choline, a nutrient
that is getting attention as a powerhouse in boosting brain
health. Eggs are the richest source of B vitamins,
especially vitamin B6 and B12. These vitamins are
involved in better brain functioning and making good
communication between brain cells.

Avocado Toast:

Serves: 2

Ingredients

- 1 avocado peeled and seeded
- 2tbsp. chopped cilantro
- ½ lemon squeezed
- 2 slice whole grain bread
- 2 eggs poached

Instructions

- Mix all the ingredients (avocado, lime juice, cilantro and spices) in a bowl.
- Spread mixture on the toast and top with poached eggs.

BON APPETITE!

Avocado Toast

NUTRITION FACTS 1 serving

Calories: 164.5kcals| Carbohydrates: 9.6g| Protein: 2g | F
at: 7.35g | Saturated
Fat: 2.1g | Cholesterol: 0mg | Sodium: 8mg | Potassium: 5
12.5mg | Fiber: 6.8g

HEALTH BENEFITS: Avocados are a rich source of vitamins C, E, K and B6 as well as riboflavin, niacin, folate, pantothenic acid, magnesium and potassium. They also provide lutein, beta carotene and omega 3 fatty acids.

Eggs contain choline, a nutrient that is getting attention as a powerhouse in boosting brain health. eggs are the richest source of B vitamins especially vitamin B6 and B12. These vitamins are involved in better brain functioning and making good communication between brain cells.

Breakfast Tacos

Serves: 2
Ingredients

- 2 eggs
- 2 corn tortillas
- ¼ cup of black beans
- 1 slice of cheese
- ¼ cup chopped spinach
- 1tbsp. chopped onion
- ¼ avocado
- Garlic powder, black pepper, salt to taste

Instructions

- Mix chopped spinach, eggs and onion in a bowl.
- You can cook eggs either on stove or in microwave. Scramble eggs on the pan and melt pepperjack cheese atop the egg mixture.
- Heat up the tortillas on stovetop, then spread beans and eggs on tortillas. Top with a few chunks of avocados & mushrooms (optional).
- Sprinkle garlic powder, salt and pepper to taste.

Breakfast Tacos

NUTRITION FACTS 1 serving

Calories: 262kcals| Carbohydrates: 26.4g| Protein: 16.4g |
Fat: 10.25g | Saturated
Fat: 4.25g | Cholesterol: 224mg | Sodium: 162.5mg | Pota
ssium: 508.5mg | Fiber: 5.4g

HEALTH BENEFITS: Eggs are the richest source of B
vitamins, especially vitamin B6 and B12. These vitamins
are involved in better brain functioning and making good
communication between brain cells. On the other hand,
spinach is rich in iron, vitamin K and vitamin A which is
involved in blood clotting, epithelialization and oxygen
transport. It improves the oxygen carrying capacity of
blood to brain and indirectly enhance brain functions.

Banana Cinnamon Oatmeal:

Serves: 1

Ingredients

- 1 cup rolled oats
- 2 cup plain unsweetened almond milk
- 1 medium banana
- ½ tsp. vanilla extract
- ½ tsp. ground cinnamon
- Pinch of salt

Instructions

- Combine all ingredients in a small saucepan and turn heat up to medium and bring it to boil.
- Turn the heat down to low and continually stir the material for 3-5 minutes as the oatmeal cooks and thickens.
- Once the oatmeal is at the desired consistency. Turn off the flame and serve it.

Banana Cinnamon Oatmeal

NUTRITION FACTS 1 serving

Calories: 203kcals| Carbohydrates: 27.5g| Protein: 14g | F
at: 4.2g | Saturated
Fat: 2.4g | Cholesterol: 14mg | Sodium: 173mg | Potassiu
m: 725mg | Fiber: 2.3g

HEALTH BENEFITS: Antioxidant flavonoids found in
bananas are also far less likely to cause heart disease and
brain disorders. Bananas contain several antioxidant
flavonoids, but catechins stand out. They have been
associated with several positive health effects, including
a decreased risk of heart disease and more.

Wild Omelet:

Serves: 1

Ingredients

- 2 eggs
- 1 pint milk
- 1/3 cup wild lox salmon
- 1 cup chopped baby spinach
- 1/3 cup diced tomatoes

Instructions

- Whisk together eggs, milk and a pinch of salt in a bowl.
- Place a non-stick pan on medium heat. Coat the pan with butter or grass-fed ghee spray.
- Add the mixture to the pan.
- Top with lox salmon and spinach
- Turn the heat down to low and lightly wrap foil on the top of the pan. Cook for 4 minutes or until the omelet has set.
- Remove foil and slide omelet onto a plate. Top with tomatoes and parsley.

Wild Omelet

NUTRITION FACTS 1 serving

Calories: 263kcals| Carbohydrates: 5.44g| Protein: 26.64g | Fat: 14.24g | Saturated Fat: 4.1g | Cholesterol: 45mg | Sodium: 355mg | Potassium: 717mg | Fiber: 1.4g

HEALTH BENEFITS: Eggs contain choline, a nutrient that is getting attention as a powerhouse in boosting brain health. Eggs are the richest source of B vitamins, especially vitamin B6 and B12. These vitamins are involved in better brain functioning and making good communication between brain cells.

2 LUNCHES

Lunch, the midday respite, offers a delicious pause in the rhythm of our day. It's a moment to refuel and recharge, to gather with colleagues or find solace in a quiet corner, and to indulge in culinary delights that satisfy both our hunger and our senses.

As the clock strikes noon, the anticipation builds. The aroma of savory dishes wafts through the air, enticing our taste buds and awakening our appetites. Whether it's a leisurely affair or a swift grab-and-go, lunch presents an opportunity to take a break from our tasks, nourishing both our bodies and our minds.

Lunchtime spreads offer a delightful array of options. From vibrant salads bursting with fresh greens and vibrant vegetables, to hearty sandwiches stacked with layers of flavorful fillings, to comforting bowls of steaming soups, lunch caters to our cravings and provides sustenance for the remainder of the day.

It's a time for social connection as we gather with colleagues, friends, or loved ones to share a meal and engage in lively conversations. The clinking of cutlery, the laughter, and the exchange of ideas create a vibrant atmosphere, fostering camaraderie and building bonds over shared experiences and a mutual love for good food.

For some, lunch is an opportunity to explore new flavors and culinary adventures. It's a chance to venture beyond the familiar, to seek out hidden gems in the local food scene or experiment with homemade creations. With each bite, we embark on a sensory journey, discovering the intricate balance of flavors, the interplay of textures, and the artistry of gastronomy.

But lunch is not just about sustenance or socialization. It's a vital pause, a chance to rejuvenate and recharge. As we savor our midday meal, we give ourselves permission to take a step back, to breathe, and to find a moment of solace amidst the demands of our day. It's a reminder that self-care and nourishment are essential ingredients for a balanced and fulfilling life.

So, let us embrace the beauty of lunch, whether it's a lavish affair or a simple moment of quiet reflection. Let us relish the flavors, the company, and the respite it brings. In this transient interlude, we find sustenance for our bodies and a sanctuary for our souls, preparing us to tackle the rest of the day with renewed energy and a satisfied spirit.

Salmon Stuffed Avocados:

Serves: 4

Ingredients

- ½ cup plain yogurt
- ½ cup diced celery
- 2tbsp. fresh parsley
- 1 tbsp. lime juice
- 2tsp. mayonnaise
- 5oz salmon, steamed
- 2 avocados
- Sea salt, pepper as per taste

Instructions

- Mix yogurt, diced celery, parsley, lime juice and mayonnaise in a bowl.
- Add steamed salmon in the form of small chunks or shredded in this mixture.
- Cut avocados into two halves lengthwise, scoop out 1tbsp of avocado from each half and mix in the salmon material.
- Fill each half of avocado with prepared salmon and vegetable mixture.

Salmon Stuffed Avocados

NUTRITION FACTS 1 serving

Calories: 242kcals| Carbohydrates: 11.7g| Protein: 80.17g | Fat: 17.8g | Saturated Fat: 2.9g | Cholesterol: 18.25 mg | Sodium: 67.75mg | Potassium: 742.25mg | Fiber: 6.9g

HEALTH BENEFITS: Salmon is rich in omega-3 fatty acids which help in improving cognitive development. It is packed with flavonoids, phytochemicals that help improve BDNF which enhances neuroplasticity and helps lower insulin spike in diabetic patients. Avocados are a rich source of vitamins C, E, K and B6 as well as riboflavin, niacin, folate, pantothenic acid, magnesium and potassium. They also provide lutein, beta carotene and omega 3 fatty acids.

Tuna Melt Sandwich:

Serves: 2
Ingredients

- 7 oz tuna (steamed)
- 1 small stalk celery
- 1 spring onion
- 3 tbsp. Greek yogurt
- 4 slices whole grain bread
- 2 slice cheddar cheese
- Salt and pepper as per required

Instructions

- Cut down steamed tuna into small chunks or you can shred it.
- Chop up celery and spring onion. Mix chopped vegetables, shredded tuna and Greek yogurt.
- Spread mixture on the bread and top with slice of cheddar cheese.
- Brush grill pan with 1tbsp. of extra virgin olive oil and grill sandwiches.

Tuna Melt Sandwich

NUTRITION FACTS 1 serving

Calories: 479.5kcals| Carbohydrates: 48.4g| Protein: 38g |
Fat: 15.146g | Saturated
Fat: 6.8g | Cholesterol: 74mg | Sodium: 537mg | Potassiu
m: 799.5mg | Fiber: 5.8g

HEALTH BENEFITS: Fishes like salmon and tuna are
rich in omega-3 fatty acids which help in improving
cognitive development. It is packed with flavonoids,
phytochemicals that help improve BDNF which enhances
neuroplasticity and helps lower insulin spike in diabetic
patients.

Shakshuka and Multigrain Bread:

Serves: 2

Ingredients

- 2tbsp. olive oil
- 1 medium red onion
- ½ bell pepper
- 2tsp. paprika
- 1tsp. cumin
- 2 garlic cloves
- 3 large eggs
- 3 cherry tomatoes
- 2 slice multigrain bread

Instructions

- Heat pan and add olive oil with chopped bell pepper and onion. Cook it for 5 minutes until the onion looks translucent. Add garlic and spices according to your taste.
- Pour chopped tomatoes and make it smooth with the help of large spoon. Bring the sauce to the simmer.

- Use a large spoon to make small wells for eggs in the sauce and crack the eggs into each well.
- Cover the pan and cook for 5-8 minutes or until eggs look done as you like. Garnish with chopped cilantro and parsley.

BON APPETITE!

NUTRITION FACTS 1 serving

Calories: 489kcals| Carbohydrates: 8.1g| Protein: 19.4g | Fat: 42.9g | Saturated
Fat: 4.6g | Cholesterol: 634mg | Sodium: 212mg | Potassium: 302mg | Fiber: 2.1g

HEALTH BENEFITS: Eggs are the richest source of B vitamins, especially vitamin B6 and B12. These vitamins are involved in better brain functioning and making good communication between brain cells. On the other hand, spinach is rich in iron, vitamin K and vitamin A which is involved in blood clotting, epithelialization and oxygen transport. It improves the oxygen carrying capacity of blood to brain and indirectly enhance brain functions.

Turkey Cobb Salad:

Serves: 3

Ingredients

- 2 tbsp. extra virgin olive oil
- 2tsp. mustard sauce
- ¼ tsp ground pepper
- 6 cups chopped lettuce
- 2 spring onions
- ½ cup cherry tomatoes
- 1 cup halved and sliced cucumber
- 3oz turkey
- 2 boiled eggs, chopped
- ½ cup cheddar cheese

Instructions

- Heat the pan and add olive oil. Add chopped lettuce, cherry tomatoes, spring onion and cook it for 1-2 minutes. Add cucumber and set this material aside.

- Steam turkey and shred it or divide it into smaller chunks.
- Whisk mustard sauce, vinegar, ground pepper, and other sauces of your own taste with boiled, chopped eggs. Mix it well and add it into the mixture of green vegetables.
- Top the mixture with chunks of steamed turkey and cheddar cheese.

BON APPETITE!

NUTRITION FACTS 1 serving

Calories: 267kcals| Carbohydrates: 8.13g| Protein: 15.37g | Fat: 10.48g | Saturated
Fat: 5.16g | Cholesterol: 172.6mg | Sodium: 513mg | Potassium: 466.3mg | Fiber: 2.5g

HEALTH BENEFITS: Turkey has high content of tryptophan an amino acid that helps increase serotonin levels in the brain leading to better sleep quality, improved focus and concentration levels throughout the day.

Avocado Egg Sandwich:

Serves: 2
Ingredients

- ½ ripe avocado
- 1 ½ lime juice
- 1tsp. avocado oil
- 3 hard-boiled eggs, chopped
- ¼ cup chopped celery
- 2 lettuce leaves
- 4 slice whole grain bread
- 1tbsp. fresh chives

Instructions

- Scoop out avocados.
- Mix scooped avocado, lime juice, boiled and chopped eggs, celery, and avocado oil in a bowl.
- Toast bread in a toaster or on grilled pan. Place lettuce leaves on one side of the sandwich and spread avocado mixture on the other side.

BON APPETITE!

Avocado Egg Sandwich

NUTRITION FACTS 1 serving

Calories: 409kcals| Carbohydrates: 52.9g| Protein:8.8 g |
Fat: 19.8g | Saturated
Fat: 2.6g | Cholesterol: 0mg | Sodium: 382.5mg | Potassiu
m: 2791.5mg | Fiber: 9.25g

HEALTH BENEFITS: Avocados are a rich source of
vitamins C, E, K and B6 as well as riboflavin, niacin,
folate, pantothenic acid, magnesium and potassium. They
also provide lutein, beta carotene and omega 3 fatty
acids.

White Bean Soup:

Serves: 4

Ingredients

- 200g northern beans
- ½ tbsp. olive oils
- 1 cup diced onion
- ½ cup diced carrot
- ½ cup diced celery
- 1tbsp. fresh garlic
- 2 cups chicken broth (reduced sodium)
- 2 cups water
- 1 dried bay leaf
- 1 tomato diced
- Salt and pepper as per taste

Instructions

- Rinse beans under cold water and transfer it to a large bowl. Add 2cups of water, cover it with a piece of cloth and soak it overnight.

- Heat oil in a large pot. Add onion, carrots, celery and cook until starts softening. Stir in garlic and cook until fragrant.
- Stir in broth, water, the soaked beans, tomatoes and bay leaves. Increase heat to high, bring to boil, and cook for 5 minutes. Reduce heat to low, partially cover and simmer until the beans are nearly tender.
- Serve with slice of multigrain bread. (optional)

BON APPETITE!

NUTRITION FACTS 1 serving

Calories: 470kcals| Carbohydrates: 74g| Protein: 23.28g | Fat: 10.76g | Saturated
Fat: 0.15g | Cholesterol: 0mg | Sodium: 264.8mg | Potassi um: 497.5mg | Fiber: 4.6g

HEALTH BENEFITS: These beans are rich in iron and protect against iron deficiency anemia and improve the oxygen carrying capacity of blood towards brain.

Avocado Hummus:

Serves: 1

Ingredients

- ½ cup chickpeas
- 1 avocado
- ¼ tahini
- ½ lime squeeze
- 1tsp. olive oil

Instructions

- Combine chickpeas, avocados, tahini, lime juice, garlic, olive oil and cumin in the bowl of a food processor and season with salt. Blend it until smooth.
- Pour mixture into a serving bowl and garnish with cilantro and red pepper flakes. Drizzle with more olive oil as you like and serve.

BON APPETITE!

Avocado Hummus

NUTRITION FACTS 1 serving

Calories: 603kcals| Carbohydrates: 45.8g| Protein: 14.4g |
 Fat: 43.9g | Saturated
Fat: 5.5g | Cholesterol: 0mg | Sodium: 213mg | Potassium
: 1399mg | Fiber: 21.3g

HEALTH BENEFITS: Avocados are rich source of
vitamins C, E, K and B6 as well as riboflavin, niacin,
folate, pantothenic acid, magnesium and potassium. They
also provide lutein, beta carotene and omega 3 fatty
acids. Chickpeas are protein rich and packed with
beneficial phytochemicals (phytoestrogens). These
phytochemicals include zeaxanthin, catty chins that help
in reduction of free radicals and improve nerve
transmission. They have low glycemic index and hence
are good for the health of diabetic patients.

Chicken Burrito Bowl:

Serves: 4
Ingredients

- 1tbsp. finely chopped peppers
- 1tbsp. extra virgin olive oil
- ½ tsp garlic powder

- ½ ground cumin
- 400g skinless chicken
- 2 cups quinoa (cooked)
- 2cups shredded lettuce
- 1 cup canned pinto beans
- 1 ripe avocado diced
- ¼ cup shredded cheddar

Instructions

- Pre-heat broiler. Combine oil, garlic powder and cumin in a small bowl. Oil the grill rack. Season chicken with salt.
- Grill chicken for 5 minutes. Turn, brush with chipotle glaze and continue cooking until an

instant read thermometer inserted in the thickest part registers 165 F. transfer to a clean bowl. Chop chicken into small chunks.

- Assemble each burrito bowl with ½ cup quinoa, ½ cup chickpeas, ½ cup lettuce, ¼ cup beans, ¼ avocado and 1 tbsp. of cheddar cheese.
- Serve it with lime wedge (optional)

BON APPETITE!

NUTRITION FACTS 1 serving

Calories: 534kcals| Carbohydrates: 57.14g| Protein: 40.3g | Fat: 13.25g | Saturated
Fat: 3.12g | Cholesterol: 65.5mg | Sodium: 278mg | Potas sium: 1442.7mg | Fiber: 12.75g

HEALTH BENEFITS: Quinoa is high in fiber, which helps in getting rid of CVDs and other metabolic disorders by lowering cholesterol and glucose levels. It has a high capacity to carry oxygen to the brain because it is rich in iron. It also contains riboflavin (Vitamin B2), which keeps brain and muscle cells healthy.

Lettuce Wrap:

Serves: 1

Ingredients

- ¼ cup plain yogurt
- 1 tbsp. mayonnaise
- ½ tsp. mustard sauce
- 2 stalks of celery
- 2 tbsp. chopped red onion
- 2-3 large iceberg lettuce leaves
- 2 carrots and cut into sticks

Instructions

- Whisk yogurt, mayonnaise, mustard, salt and pepper in a medium bowl.
- Chop eggs and transfer to bowl. Cut lettuce leaves in half and double layer them to make 2 lettuces wrap. Divide the egg salad among the wraps and top with basil. Serve with carrot sticks on the side.

BON APPETITE!

Lettuce Wrap

NUTRITION FACTS 1 serving

Calories: 152kcals| Carbohydrates: 20.8g| Protein: 4.8g |
Fat: 6g | Saturated
Fat: 1.3g | Cholesterol: 1.3mg | Sodium: 262mg | Potassiu
m: 645mg | Fiber: 4.2g

HEALTH BENEFITS: Lettuce is a fair source of
folate, which is needed for healthy cells of brain. During
pregnancy folate is very important for spine development
and excellent baby growth.

Black Bean Salad:

Serves: 4

Ingredients

- ½ cup thin sliced onion
- 1 medium ripe avocado
- ¼ cups cilantro leaves
- ¼ cup lime juice
- 1 clove garlic
- 1 diced and halved cucumber
- 2 cups frozen corn kernels
- 1 pint grape tomatoes
- 1 can black beans, rinsed

Instructions

- Place onion in a bowl and cover with cold water. Set it aside.
- Combine avocado, cilantro, lime juice, oil, garlic and salt in a mini food processor. Process, scraping down the sides as needed, until smooth and creamy.
- Combine salad greens (tomatoes, corn and beans) in a large bowl. Drain the onions and add to the bowl, along with the avocado dressing.

Black Bean Salad

NUTRITION FACTS 1 serving

Calories: 209.25kcals| Carbohydrates: 30.8g| Protein: 7.2 g | Fat: 8.25g | Saturated Fat: 1.22g | Cholesterol: 0mg | Sodium: 246.25mg | Potassium: 676.25mg | Fiber:9.8 g

HEALTH BENEFITS: Protein is essential to our body's function and growth. Black beans are rich in protein and packed with beneficial amino acids, mainly tryptophan. It is involved in memory and cognition.

3 SNACKS

Snacks, those delightful morsels of joy, add a burst of excitement to our daily routines. They are the tantalizing interludes that punctuate our day, providing moments of indulgence and satisfaction when we need them most. Whether it's a quick bite between meals or a delightful treat to accompany our activities, snacks hold the power to uplift our spirits and satiate our cravings.

Snacks come in all shapes, sizes, and flavors, catering to our individual tastes and desires. They range from the crispy crunch of potato chips to the sweet allure of chocolate bars, from the refreshing tang of fruits to the savory temptation of cheese and crackers. With each bite, we embark on a journey of flavors, a brief escape from the ordinary.

Beyond their gustatory pleasures, snacks offer us a moment of respite, a chance to pause and recharge. They are the fuel that keeps us going, providing a burst of energy to power through the day's demands. Whether we reach for a handful of nuts or a grab-and-go granola bar, snacks bridge the gap between meals, keeping us fueled and focused.

Snacks also carry a sense of nostalgia and comfort. They

evoke memories of childhood treats, late-night cravings, and cherished moments of togetherness. The act of enjoying a snack can transport us back to carefree days and bring a smile to our faces, reminding us of simple pleasures and the joy of savoring the little things in life.

Moreover, snacks have become a canvas for creativity and innovation. From artisanal creations that showcase unique flavor combinations to healthier alternatives that cater to dietary preferences, snacks have evolved into a realm of endless possibilities. They allow us to explore new tastes, embrace culinary trends, and even express our own culinary prowess through homemade delights.

So, let us celebrate the magic of snacks. May we delight in their flavors, appreciate the joy they bring, and relish the moments of indulgence they offer. Whether we enjoy them on the go, at work, or in the comfort of our homes, let snacks be a source of pleasure, nourishment, and a reminder to savor life's little pleasures one bite at a time.

Cucumber Boats:

Serves: 1

Ingredients

- 4 small cucumbers
- 100g cherry tomatoes
- 50g kalamata olives
- 1 small red onion
- 50g feta cheese
- 1 tsp. dried oregano
- 3tbsp. Greek yogurt

Instructions

- Cut down all the cucumbers in a length wise position.
- Remove seeds with the help of spoon or knife.
- Mix all the roughly chopped vegetables in a bowl. Add Greek yogurt with ½ lemon squeezed.
- Fill cucumbers with mixture and top with chunks of feta cheese.

BON APPETITE!

Cucumber Boats

NUTRITION FACTS 1 serving

Calories: 509kcals| Carbohydrates: 63.59g| Protein: 20.15 g | Fat: 25.5g | Saturated Fat: 12.2g | Cholesterol: 74mg | Sodium: 1179mg | Potassium: 2280mg | Fiber: 9.8g

HEALTH BENEFITS: Consumption of green vegetables like cucumber, spinach, parsley, kale and Greek yogurt help slowing the decline in cognitive abilities with older age, perhaps due to neuroprotective functions of lutein, folate, beta carotene and phylloquinone. These help in improvement of BDNF that increases neuroplasticity.

Fruit and Nut Salad:

Serves: 1

Ingredients

- 1 medium size apple
- ½ pomegranate
- 3-4 walnuts
- 12 almonds
- 1tsp. honey
- Pinch of cinnamon powder

Instructions

- Dice all the fruit in a bowl.
- Crush nuts (walnuts, almonds)
- Mix both ingredients. Add honey and cinnamon powder.

BON APPETITE!

Fruit and Nut Salad

NUTRITION FACTS 1 serving

Calories: 153kcals| Carbohydrates: 21.15g| Protein: 2.9g |
Fat: 7.7g | Saturated
Fat: 0.6g | Cholesterol: 0mg | Sodium: 1.5mg | Potassium:
254.5mg | Fiber: 3.15g

HEALTH BENEFITS: A diet consisting of 1 serving of
almonds per day can help in reduction of depression and
anxiety especially with diabetic patients. An almond-
based low carbohydrate diet improves depression and
glucometabolic in patients with type 2 diabetes through
modulating gut microbiota and GLP-1: a randomized
controlled trial. Numerous studies have connected higher
vitamin E intake with reduced risk of cancer, Alzheimer's
disease, and heart disease.

Dark Chocolate and Nut Smoothie:

Serves: 1

Ingredients

- 1 or 2 bars of dark chocolate
- 6 almonds
- 3 walnuts
- 1 cup Greek yogurt
- Water to thin consistency

Instructions

- Add all the ingredients in a high-powered blender and blend it until smooth.
- Serve it with 1tsp. of chocolate syrup and crushed nuts topping.

BON APPETITE!

Dark Chocolate and Nut Smoothie

NUTRITION FACTS 1 serving

Calories:568.5 kcals| Carbohydrates: 38.6g| Protein: 13.7 g | Fat: 43.5g | Saturated Fat: 22.5g | Cholesterol: 83mg | Sodium: 139mg | Potassium: 1045.5mg | Fiber: 3.5g

HEALTH BENEFITS: Dark chocolate is a powerful source of antioxidants. ORAC stands for oxygen radical absorbent capacity. It measures the antioxidant activity of foods. It is loaded with organic compounds that are biologically active and function as antioxidants. These include polyphenols, flavanols and catechins among others. According to research, polyphenols help lowers LDL when combined with other foods like almonds and cocoa.

Anti-Inflammatory Salad:

Serves: 1

Ingredients

- 5-6 strawberries
- 2 medium dates
- 1 peach
- ½ cup Greek yogurt
- 1tsp. honey (optional)

Instructions

- Dice peach and strawberries in a bowl and chop dates into small chunks.
- Mix all the ingredients with Greek yogurt and top it with tsp. of honey or dark chocolate syrup.

BON APPETITE!

Anti-Inflammatory Salad

NUTRITION FACTS 1 serving

Calories: 230.5kcals| Carbohydrates: 55.8g| Protein: 6.8g | Fat: 11.38g | Saturated Fat: 6.8g | Cholesterol: 41.5mg | Sodium: 67mg | Potassium: 799mg | Fiber: 5.9g

HEALTH BENEFITS: This salad is packed with all kinds of ingredients that reduce chronic inflammation and help lower oxidative stress.

Beetroot and Clementine Juice:

Serves: 1

Ingredients

- 5 medium size clementine
- 2 medium beetroots
- ½ lemon squeezed
- Pinch of sea salt
- 2-3 mint leaves
- 1 tsp of sugar

Instructions

- Peel clementine and separate slices in a bowl.
- Dice beetroot and blend all the ingredients in high powered blender.
- Strain juice in a jug. Add lemon juice, sea salt, mint leaves and table sugar. Blend it again until smooth.
- Cool it with ice or in refrigerator and serve.

BON APPETITE!

Beetroot and Clementine Juice

NUTRITION FACTS 1 serving

Calories: 245kcals| Carbohydrates: 60g| Protein: 5.7g | Fat: 0.78g | Saturated
Fat: 0g | Cholesterol: 0mg | Sodium: 132mg | Potassium: 1188mg | Fiber: 10.9g

HEALTH BENEFITS: Mental and cognitive health declines about 5% each year after 50 years of age, which may increase the risk of neurodegenerative disorders like dementia. The nitrates in beetroot are beneficial for improving brain function by promoting the dilation of blood vessels and thus increasing blood flow to the brain.

4 DINNERS

Dinner, the culmination of the day's events, beckons us to gather around the table and indulge in a feast of flavors, stories, and shared moments. It is a ritual that transcends mere sustenance, transforming a simple meal into a celebration of nourishment and connection.

As the sun sets, the ambiance shifts, and a sense of anticipation fills the air. Dinner is a time to unwind, to recount the day's triumphs and challenges, and to forge deeper connections with those we hold dear. The table becomes a stage where conversations flow, laughter echoes, and bonds strengthen over the shared experience of a meal.

Dinner offers a culinary symphony, a harmonious ensemble of tastes and textures that delights our palates and ignites our senses. It is a moment of culinary exploration, where dishes blend tradition with innovation, transporting us to distant lands and evoking cherished memories. From savory roasts and fragrant stews to vibrant salads and delicate desserts, each dish tells a story, inviting us to savor the rich tapestry of flavors.

Beyond the culinary artistry, dinner nourishes our bodies and minds. It provides sustenance that revitalizes our energy, allowing us to recharge and prepare for the adventures that lie ahead. A well-balanced dinner fuels our bodies, providing the nutrients and vitality needed to embrace life's challenges with vigor and grace.

Dinner also carries an inherent sense of gratitude. It is a time to appreciate the bounties of the earth and the hands that have cultivated them. Whether we gather around a homemade meal or savor the creations of talented chefs, dinner reminds us of the interconnectedness between food, nature, and the labor of love that brings it to our plates.

In a world that often feels fast-paced and fragmented, dinner serves as an anchor—a sacred pause that brings us back to ourselves and to each other. It is a reminder that amidst the chaos, we can find solace, nourishment, and connection in the simple act of breaking bread together.

So, let us embrace the enchantment of dinner. Let us revel in the symphony of flavors, the joy of shared conversations, and the warmth of communal dining. May we approach each dinner with gratitude, savoring the flavors, the connections, and the moments of respite it brings. In this cherished tradition, let us find sustenance for our bodies and nourishment for our souls, as we celebrate the beauty of food, fellowship, and the richness of life itself.

Pan Salmon & Sautéed Vegetables:

Serves: 4

Ingredients

- 3 tbsp. Greek yogurt
- 2 medium sweet potatoes (peeled & diced)
- 4tsp.olive oil
- 4 cups broccoli florets
- 4 salmon fillet
- ¼ cup feta cheese
- ½ cup chopped cilantro

Instructions

- Pre heat oven to 400 degrees F. line a large, rimmed baking sheet with foil and coat with cooking spray.
- Combine Greek yogurt and chili powder in a small bowl. Set this aside.

- Toss sweet potatoes with 2 tsp. olive oil and pinch of salt and ground pepper in a medium bowl.
- Spread the material on baking sheet. Toss broccoli and add salt and pepper in the same bowl.
- Remove the baking sheet from oven, stir the sweet potatoes and move them to the sides of the pan. Spread broccoli on either side, among sweet potatoes.
- Spread 2tbsp. of yogurt mixture on salmon. Bake it until sweet potatoes seem done and salmon flakes easily with fork.
- Divide salmon among 4 plates and top with cheese and cilantro.

BON APPETITE!

NUTRITION FACTS 1 serving

Calories: 261.5kcals| Carbohydrates: 19.78g| Protein: 16.11g | Fat: 13.6g | Saturated Fat: 2.7g | Cholesterol: 26mg | Sodium: 405mg | Potassium: 823.7mg | Fiber: 8g

HEALTH BENEFITS: Salmon is rich in omega-3 fatty acids which helps in improving cognitive development. It is packed with flavonoids, phytochemicals that help improve BDNF which enhances neuroplasticity and helps lower insulin spike in diabetic patients.

Chicken Enchilada:

Serves: 6

Ingredients

- 2tbsp. olive oil
- 1 cup fresh corn kernel
- ½ cup diced green bell pepper
- ½ cup diced red bell pepper
- ½ cup diced onion
- 200g baby spinach
- 2 ½ cups shredded cooked chicken breast
- 100g green enchilada sauce
- 1 cup fresh salsa
- 5-6 corn tortillas
- 1 ½ cups shredded cheese
- 1 cup chopped cherry tomatoes
- ¼ cup carrots

Instructions

- Pre heat oven to 350 degrees F.

- Heat oil in a large ovenproof skillet. Add corn, green and red bell pepper, onion and stir it occasionally, until charred. Gradually add spinach in batches, cook, stirring frequently, until wilted, 1-2 minutes.
- Stir in chicken, enchilada sauce and salsa until combined. Gently stir in tortilla strips. Sprinkle with cheese. Transfer to the oven and bake until bubbly.
- Top with cilantro, tomatoes and radishes (optional)

BON APPETITE!

NUTRITION FACTS 1 serving

Calories: 239kcals| Carbohydrates: 19.14g| Protein: 25.9g | Fat: 9.3g | Saturated Fat: 4.7g | Sodium:45.6 mg | Potassium: 400mg | Fiber: 3. 3g

HEALTH BENEFITS: Vegetables like bell pepper and carrots are rich in vitamin C and vitamin A. It has anti-inflammatory properties and prevents free radicals from oxidation which improves brain health.

Coconut Curry with Whole Grain Bread:

Serves: 4

Ingredients

- 2 tbsp. olive oil
- 1 medium onion
- 2 medium stalks of celery
- 3 scallions
- 2 garlic cloves
- 2 tsp. curcumin
- 4 cups peeled butternut squash
- 4 cups vegetable broth
- 1 cup coconut milk
- 1 cup chickpeas
- ½ cup unsalted pepitas

Instructions

- Wash and soak chickpeas overnight. Heat pan and add olive oil. Add chopped garlic cloves, medium onion, stalk of celery and spring onion. Sautéed for 2-3 minutes.

- Add vegetable broth in a pot and add vegetable mixture in it. Add butter nut squash, coconut milk and chickpeas in broth. Cook until smooth and thickened.
- Enjoy it with bread. (optional)

BON APPETITE!

NUTRITION FACTS 1 serving

Calories: 321.25kcals| Carbohydrates: 22.5g| Protein: 8.7 g | Fat: 25.5g | Saturated
Fat: 0g | Cholesterol: 0mg | Sodium: 124.5mg | Potassium : 556.7mg | Fiber: 2.4g

HEALTH BENEFITS: Chickpeas are protein rich and packed with beneficial phytochemicals (phytoestrogens). These phytochemicals include zeaxanthin, catty chins that help in reduction of free radicals and improve nerve transmission. They have low glycemic index and hence are good for the health of diabetic patients.

Mixed Vegetable & Salmon Rice:

Serves: 1

Ingredients

- 100g white rice (boiled)
- 1 small bell pepper (green)
- 1 cherry tomato
- 1 spring onion
- 3oz salmon (steamed & shredded)
- ¼ cabbage
- 1 small carrot (matchstick cut)
- 1 tbsp. olive oil

Instructions

- Add 1 tbsp. of olive oil to a pan. Heat on low flame add all the diced vegetables in the pan.
- Sautee vegetables for 5-6 minutes and add spices and condiments according to your taste. Add steamed, shredded salmon to vegetable mixture.
- Mix white boiled rice in vegetable mixture and mix well.
- Serve it in plate with hot sauce (optional)

BON APPETITE!

Mixed Vegetable & Salmon Rice

NUTRITION FACTS 1 serving

Calories: 453kcals| Carbohydrates: 48.1g| Protein: 25.07g | Fat: 19.65g | Saturated Fat: 1g | Cholesterol: 38mg | Sodium: 455mg | Potassium: 938mg | Fiber: 5.4g

HEALTH BENEFITS: Vegetables like bell pepper, carrots, spring onion and broccoli are rich in vitamin C and vitamin A. It has anti-inflammatory properties and prevents free radicals from oxidation which improves brain health. Salmon is rich in omega-3 fatty acids which helps in improving cognitive development. It is packed with flavonoids, phytochemicals that help improve BDNF which enhances neuroplasticity and help lower insulin spike in diabetic patients.

Steamed Fish with Mint Greek Yogurt:

Serves: 2

Ingredients

- 2 salmon fillet
- 1tsp. olive oil
- 1 spring onion
- 1 spring cilantro
- 1 cup Greek yogurt

Instructions

- For the steamed salmon. Fill a large pot with steamer tray halfway up with water and bring to a boil.
- Meanwhile, find a heatproof plate or nonreactive cake or pie pan that will hold the salmon fillets and will also fit in the steamer tray about 1 inch left round edges. Toss half of the white scallion strips into pan.
- Place salmon fillet on top.
- Transfer the pan to the steamer tray. Cover the pot, cook until fish is cooked, 8-10 minutes.

- Transfer the fish to a platter and pour lime juice on the top. Garnish with chopped scallion and cilantro

BON APPETITE!

NUTRITION FACTS 1 serving

Calories: 246kcals| Carbohydrates: 6.6g| Protein: 17.25g |
 Fat: 16.3g | Saturated
Fat: 7.55g | Cholesterol: 67mg | Sodium: 93mg | Potassiu
m: 449mg | Fiber: 0.2g

HEALTH BENEFITS: Salmon is rich in omega-3 fatty acids which helps in improving cognitive development. It is packed with flavonoids, phytochemicals that help improve BDNF which enhances neuroplasticity and helps lower insulin spike in diabetic patients.

Vegetable and Lentil Soup:

Serves: 4

Ingredients

- 1 onion diced, 3 garlic cloves, 3 stalks celery
- 1 tsp. oregano
- 1 tsp. curry powder, 1tsp. curcumin, ½ tsp. red pepper
- 4 cups vegetable broth
- 1 diced tomato
- 1 cup lentils
- ¼ cup frozen peas
- Handful of spinach

Instructions

- Sauté all the vegetables in a large pot with splash of water on medium flame. Add garlic, spices and salt and cook another minute.
- Add all other ingredients (tomatoes, lentils, vegetable broth), bring it to boil. Reduce heat to low and let gently simmer for about 20 minutes, until lentils are soft. Add spinach and stir for a few minutes. Add frozen peas, it helps cool down.
- Season with additional salt and pepper.

BON APPETITE!

Vegetable and Lentil Soup

NUTRITION FACTS 1 serving

Calories: 218kcals| Carbohydrates: 38.7g| Protein: 15.6g |
Fat: 0.6g | Saturated
Fat: 0g | Cholesterol: 0mg | Sodium: 49mg | Potassium: 7
25.7mg | Fiber: 16.4g

HEALTH BENEFITS: Lentils are protein rich and
packed with beneficial phytochemicals (phytoestrogens).
These phytochemicals include zeaxanthin, catty chins
that help in reduction of free radicals and improve nerve
transmission. They have low glycemic index and hence
are good for the health of diabetic patients. Vegetables
like carrots, spring onion and broccoli are rich in vitamin
C and vitamin A. It has anti-inflammatory properties and
prevents free radicals from oxidation which improves
brain health.

Chicken Steak with Sautéed Vegetables:

Serves: 2

Ingredients

- 200g chicken breast
- 1 tbsp olive oil
- ¼ broccoli
- ½ cucumber
- ½ carrot
- 2 garlic cloves

Instructions

- Begin by flattening your chicken breasts with a heavy mallet if needed.

- Place your chicken breasts in a medium bowl and add the marinating ingredients. Coat thoroughly.

- Marinate your chicken for 20 minutes or overnight if necessary.

- Preheat the grill pan and brush with olive oil.

- Place the chicken fillets on the grill pan and cook for 6-7 minutes per side.

- Serve with sautéed vegetables and white sauce (optional)

BON APPETITE!

NUTRITION FACTS 1 serving

Calories:275.5 kcals| Carbohydrates: 4.2g| Protein: 30.4g | Fat: 14.8g | Saturated Fat: 2.15g | Cholesterol: 83mg | Sodium: 469mg | Potassium: 429.7mg | Fiber: 1.5g

HEALTH BENEFITS: Chicken is a great source of lean protein, offers a balance of brain-healthy compounds, and is a good source of dietary choline and vitamins B6 and B12. Choline and the B vitamins have been shown to play important roles in healthy cognition and provide neuroprotective benefits.

Bean and Salmon Tostadas:

Serves: 4

Ingredients

- 8 tortillas (6'')
- 1 tsp. olive oil
- 6oz boneless salmon
- 1 avocado
- 2 tbsp. minced jalapenos
- 1 cup shredded cabbage
- 6oz black beans
- 2 spring onion
- 3bsp Greek yogurt

Instructions

- Position racks in upper and lower thirds of the oven. Preheat oven to 375degreeF.
- Coat tortillas on both sides with cooking spray. Place on 2 baking sheets. Bake it turn once, until light brown.
- Combine salmon, avocado and jalapenos in a bowl. Combine cabbage, cilantro and the pickling juice (if using) in another bowl.
- Process black beans, sour cream, and scallions in a food processor until smooth. Transfer to a

microwave safe bowl. Cover and microwave on high until hot.

- Assemble tostadas, spread each tortilla with some salmon and bean mixture and top with the cabbage salad. Serve with lime wedge if desired.

BON APPETITE!

NUTRITION FACTS 1 serving

Calories: 317.7kcals| Carbohydrates: 35.3g| Protein: 16.6 g | Fat: 13.2g | Saturated
Fat: 3g | Cholesterol: 26.7mg | Sodium: 222mg | Potassiu m: 741.5mg | Fiber: 9.9g

HEALTH BENEFITS: Salmon is rich in omega-3 fatty acids which helps in improving cognitive development. It is packed with flavonoids, phytochemicals that help improve BDNF which enhances neuroplasticity and helps lower insulin spike in diabetic patients. Avocados contain B vitamins, which have been studied for their potential role in brain health because of their role in homocysteine metabolism. An elevated homocysteine level is a risk factor for AD and dementia. B vitamins can help to lower homocysteine levels.

Lemon Garlic Fettuccine:

Serves: 1

Ingredients

- 8oz whole wheat fettuccine
- 4 tbsp. extra virgin olive oil
- 4 garlic cloves
-
- ¼ cup lemon juice

- 1 tsp. ground pepper
- 3oz skinless sardines
- ¼ cup chopped cheddar cheese

Instructions

- Bring a large pot of water to a boil. Cook pasta until just tender, 8-10 minutes or according to package directions. Drain pasta.
- Meanwhile, heat 2tbsp. of olive oil in a small non-stick pan. Add garlic, stir until fragrant. Transfer garlic and oil to a large bowl.
- Pan over medium flame. Add breadcrumbs (if using) until light brown.
- Whisk lemon juice, pepper and salt into the garlic oil. Add pasta to the bowl with sardines, parsley

and cheddar cheese. Gently stir to combine with the breadcrumbs.

BON APPETITE!

NUTRITION FACTS 1 serving

Calories: 398kcals| Carbohydrates: 43.07g| Protein: 15.3g | Fat: 19.5g | Saturated Fat: 1.9g | Cholesterol: 37.7mg | Sodium: 155.7mg | Potassium: 214mg | Fiber: 0g

HEALTH BENEFITS: Lemon and garlic are rich in phytochemicals and vitamin C (ascorbic acid). These flavonoids and phytoestrogens help in lowering blood pressure and improve oxygen carrying capacity of blood to brain.

Tuna Wrap:

Serves: 4

Ingredients

- 5oz tuna chunks
- 1/3 cup Greek yogurt mix with lime juice
- 1 spring onion
- 2 cups cooked brown rice
- 4 whole grain wraps
- 2tbsp rice vinegar
- 1 carrot
- 3 cups watercress leaves

Instructions

- Combine tuna, Greek yogurt with lime, hot sauce and scallion in a medium bowl.
- Combine rice and vinegar in a small bowl.
- Spread one fourth of the tuna mixture over wrap. Top with ½ cup rice, ¾ cup watercress, 4 avocado slices and one fourth of the carrot matchstick.
- Roll up and cut wrap in quarters or in half.
- Repeat with remaining filling and serve with soy sauce (optional).

BON APPETITE!

Tuna Wrap

NUTRITION FACTS 1 serving

Calories: 298.25kcals| Carbohydrates: 39.5g| Protein: 15.9g | Fat: 9g | Saturated Fat: 1.5g | Cholesterol: 12mg | Sodium: 545.5mg | Potassium: 604.25mg | Fiber: 7g

HEALTH BENEFITS: Tuna is packed with omega 3 and B vitamins that lower homocysteine levels. Too much homocysteine can cause brain stroke. Thus, tuna helps in improving brain health.

Bean & Barley Soup:

Serves: 6

Ingredients

- 1tbsp extra virgin olive oil
- 1 large onion
- 1 stalk celery
- 1 large carrot
- 9 cups water
- 4 cups chicken broth
- ½ cup pearl barley
- 1/3 cup dried black beans
- 1/3 cup northern beans
- 1/3 cup kidney beans
- Dried oregano, sea salt, pepper as per taste.

Instructions

- Heat oil in a Dutch oven over medium flame. Add onion, celery, carrot and cook by continuously stirring until soften. Add water, broth, barley, black beans, great northern beans, kidney beans, chili powder, cumin and oregano.
- Bring to lively simmer on high heat. Reduce heat to maintain a simmer and cook stirring occasionally, until beans are tender.
- Season with salt and serve it.

Bean & Barley Soup

NUTRITION FACTS 1 serving

Calories: 163.16kcals| Carbohydrates: 23.5g| Protein: 9.3 g | Fat: 3.6g | Saturated
Fat: 0.28g | Cholesterol: 0mg | Sodium: 2180mg | Potassi um: 571.16mg | Fiber: 5g

HEALTH BENEFITS: Lentils are protein rich and packed with beneficial phytochemicals (phytoestrogens). These phytochemicals include zeaxanthin, catty chins that help in reduction of free radicals and improve nerve transmission. They have low glycemic index and hence are good for the health of diabetic patients. Vegetables like carrots, spring onion and broccoli are rich in vitamin C and vitamin A. It has anti-inflammatory properties and prevents free radicals from oxidation which improves brain health.

Black Bean Quesadillas:

Serves: 4

Ingredients

- 1 can black beans, rinsed
- ½ cup shredded pepper jack cheese
- 4 whole wheat tortillas (8'')
- 1 avocado, diced

Instructions

- Combine beans, cheese and ¼ cup salsa (if using) in a medium bowl.
- Place tortillas on a work surface. Spread ½ cup filling on half of each tortilla. Fold tortilla in half, pressing gently to flatten.
- Heat 1 tsp. oil in a large nonstick pan or skillet over medium heat. Add 2 quesadillas and cook, turning once, cook until golden brown. Transfer to a cutting board and tent with foil to keep warm.
- Repeat with remaining material and serve with avocado and salsa (optional)

BON APPETITE!

Black Bean Quesadillas

NUTRITION FACTS 1 serving

Calories: 284kcals| Carbohydrates: 33.8g| Protein: 11.4g |
Fat: 12.6g | Saturated
Fat: 4.13g | Cholesterol: 14.7mg | Sodium: 412.7mg | Pot
assium: 525.7mg |

HEALTH BENEFITS: Black beans are protein rich and
packed with beneficial phytochemicals (phytoestrogens).
These phytochemicals include zeaxanthin, catty chins
that help in reduction of free radicals and improve nerve
transmission. They have low glycemic index and hence
are good for the health of diabetic patients. Vegetables
like carrots, spring onion and broccoli are rich in vitamin
C and vitamin A. It has anti-inflammatory properties and
prevents free radicals from oxidation which improves
brain health.

Salmon Salad Sandwich:

Serves: 4

Ingredients

- 6oz salmon boneless (steamed, shredded)
- ¼ cup minced onion
- 2tbsp. lemon juice
- 1tbsp. olive oil
- 4tbsp. cream cheese
- 4 slice whole grain bread

Instructions

- Combine salmon, onion, lemon juice, oil and pepper in a medium bowl. Spread 1 tbsp. cream cheese on each top of 2 slices of bread.
- Spread ½ cup salmon salad over the cream cheese. Top with slices of tomatoes, a piece of lettuce and another slice of bread.

BON APPETITE!

Salmon Salad Sandwich

NUTRITION FACTS 1 serving

Calories: 175kcals| Carbohydrates: 16g| Protein: 12.4g | F
at: 7.2 g | Saturated
Fat: 0.5g | Cholesterol: 19.25mg | Sodium: 170mg | Potas
sium: 393mg | Fiber: 2.7g

HEALTH BENEFITS: Salmon is rich in omega-3 fatty
acids which help in improving cognitive development. It
is packed with flavonoids, phytochemicals that help
improve BDNF which enhances neuroplasticity and helps
lower insulin spike in diabetic patients.

Tomato and Avocado Tacos:

Serves: 1

Ingredients

- 2 tortillas
- 1 avocado
- ½ cup cherry tomatoes
- 1 small red onion
- ½ lemon squeezed
- Spices, sauces as per required

Instructions

- Combine all the diced ingredients (avocado, tomato, onion) in a small bowl. Add lemon juice stir well.
- Heat up tortillas until golden brown on low flame. Fill each tortilla with half of the mixture.

BON APPETITE!

Tomato and Avocado Tacos

NUTRITION FACTS 1 serving

Calories: 548kcals| Carbohydrates: 65.9g| Protein: 11.9g |
Fat: 30.4g | Saturated
Fat: 4.36g | Cholesterol: 0mg | Sodium: 360mg | Potassiu
m: 1420mg | Fiber: 20g

HEALTH BENEFITS: Avocados contain B vitamins,
which have been studied for their potential role in brain
health because of their role in homocysteine metabolism.
An elevated homocysteine level is a risk factor for AD
and dementia. B vitamins can help to lower
homocysteine levels.

Chicken and Broccoli Pasta:

Serves: 4

Ingredients

- 2 cups unsalted chicken broth
- 2 cups water
- 8oz whole grain small shell pasta
-
- 1tbsp. olive oil
- 1 ½ Worcestershire sauce
- 1tbsp. tomato paste
- 3 garlic cloves minced
- 12oz broccoli cut into bite size pieces
- 2 cups shredded chicken breast
- ¾ cup Greek yogurt
- ¾ cup grated cheese

Instructions

- Combine broth, water, Worcestershire sauce, tomato paste, oil, pasta, garlic, pepper and salt in a large pot.
- Bring to a boil over high heat.
- Add broccoli and continue stirring to avoid pasta from sticking.

- Remove from heat, stir in chicken, yogurt and cheese.

BON APPETITE!

NUTRITION FACTS 1 serving

Calories: 482kcals| Carbohydrates: 57.6g| Protein: 35.8g | Fat: 13.6g | Saturated Fat: 5.3g | Cholesterol: 63.75mg | Sodium: 585.5mg | Pot assium: 768.5mg | Fiber: 2.2g

HEALTH BENEFITS: Chicken is rich in protein, omega-3 and B vitamins.

White Bean Gnocchi:

Serves: 4

Ingredients

- ½ cup sun dried tomatoes
- 1 packaged gnocchi
- 15oz cannellini beans
- 1/3 cup chicken broth1/3 cup heavy cream
- 1tbsp. lime juice
- 3tbsp. basil leaves

Instructions

- Heat 1tbsp. oil in a large nonstick pan over medium heat. Add gnocchi and cook. Continue stirring while cooking until plumped and starting to brown, about 5 minutes. Add beans and cook until beans become soft.
- Add the remaining 1tbsp of olive oil to pan and heat over medium flame. Add sun dried tomatoes and cook for 1 minute.
- Add broth to the pan and increase heat to high. Cook until the liquid has evaporated.

- Reduce heat to medium and stir in cream, lemon juice, salt and pepper. Add gnocchi mixture to the pan and stir to coat with the sauce. Serve topped with basil.

BON APPETITE!

NUTRITION FACTS 1 serving

Calories: 275.5kcals| Carbohydrates: 35.8g| Protein: 10.5 4g | Fat: 10.8g | Saturated
Fat: 6.4g | Cholesterol: 34.5mg | Sodium: 293.7mg | Pota ssium: 809mg | Fiber: 6.4g

HEALTH BENEFITS: Lemon is rich in vitamin C, acts as an antioxidant and helps lower free radicals. Spinach is rich in vitamin K and A, also involved in anti-inflammatory purposes and helps in improving brain health.

Lemon Chicken with Spinach:

Serves: 4

Ingredients

- 2tbsp. olive oil
- 400g boneless chicken
- 1 cup diced red bell pepper
- Ground pepper & salt as per taste
- 4 garlic cloves
- 10 cups baby spinach
- 8tsp. parmesan cheese

Instructions

- Heat oil in a large skillet over medium heat. Add chicken, bell pepper, salt, ground pepper and cook until chicken is cooked.
- Add garlic and cook stirring until fragrant.
- Add to the pan along with lemon juice, handful of spinach and cook until spinach looks wilted.
- Serve sprinkle parmesan cheese on the top.

BON APPETITE!

Lemon Chicken with Spinach

NUTRITION FACTS 1 serving

Calories: 282.75kcals| Carbohydrates: 4.92g| Protein: 32. 02g | Fat: 15.13g | Saturated Fat: 1.7g | Cholesterol: 83.25mg | Sodium: 455.5mg | Pot assium: 740mg | Fiber: 2.4g

HEALTH BENEFITS: Lemon is rich in vitamin C, acts as an antioxidant and helps lower free radicals. Spinach is rich in vitamin K and A, also involved in anti-inflammatory purposes and helps in improving brain health.

Salmon Tacos with Pineapple Salsa:

Serves: 4

Ingredients

- 1 salmon fillet
- 1tbsp olive oil
- 8 corn tortillas
- ¾ cup pineapple salsa
- Hot sauce for serving (optional)
- Spices according to your taste

Instructions

- Arrange oven rack in upper third of oven so salmon will be 2-3 inches below heat source. Pre heat broiler to high.
- Line baking sheet with foil. Lay salmon on the foil, skin-side down. Broil, rotating the pan from front to back once, until salmon is starting to brown, is opaque on the sides and the thinner parts of the fillet are sizzling.

- Sprinkle the salmon with chili powder and salt. Drizzle with tsp. of olive oil. Return to oven and continue broiling until salmon flakes and spices are browned.
- Divide salmon among tortillas and top with salsa. Garnish with cilantro and parsley (optional)

BON APPETITE!

NUTRITION FACTS 1 serving

Calories: 196.5kcals| Carbohydrates: 24.3g| Protein: 11.7 5g | Fat: 6.4g | Saturated
Fat: 0.5g | Cholesterol: 19.5mg | Sodium: 321mg | Potassi um: 381.25mg | Fiber: 3.7g

HEALTH BENEFITS: Salmon is rich in omega-3 fatty acids which help improve cognitive development, also help in improving neuroplasticity. It increases BDNF that is mostly involved in long term memory, learning and helps lower insulin spike in blood.

Chicken and Vegetable Kabab:

Serves: 2

Ingredients

- 200g chicken breast
- ½ bell pepper (green)
- 1 small carrot
- Shredded ¼ cup cabbage
- 1tbsp coconut powder

Instructions

- Boil and shred chicken breast.
- Chop all the vegetables and mix with shredded chicken.
- Add coconut powder and make definite shapes of kabab.
- Air fry kabab and serve with mint Greek yogurt.

BON APPETITE!

Chicken and Vegetable Kabab

NUTRITION FACTS 1 serving

Calories: 459kcals| Carbohydrates: 13.1g| Protein: 61.1g |
 Fat: 16.7g | Saturated
Fat: 4.4g | Cholesterol: 166mg | Sodium: 838mg | Potassi
um: 815mg | Fiber: 5.5g

HEALTH BENEFITS: Vegetables like bell pepper and
carrots are rich in vitamin C and vitamin A. It has anti-
inflammatory properties and prevents free radicals from
oxidation which improves brain health.

Chicken Quinoa Curry:

Serves: 4

Ingredients

- 1tbsp. finely chopped peppers
- 1tbsp. extra virgin olive oil
- ½ tsp garlic powder
- ½ ground cumin
- 400g skinless chicken
- 2 cups quinoa (cooked)
- 2cups shredded lettuce
- 1 cup canned pinto beans
- 1 ripe avocado diced
- ¼ cup shredded cheddar

Instructions

- Pre-heat broiler. Combine oil, garlic powder and cumin in a small bowl. Oil the grill rack. Season chicken with salt.
- Grill chicken for 5 minutes. Turn, brush with chipotle glaze and continue cooking until an instant read thermometer inserted in the thickest

part registers 165 F. transfer to a clean bowl. Chop chicken into small chunks.

- Assemble each burrito bowl with ½ cup quinoa, ½ cup chickpeas, ½ cup lettuce, ¼ cup beans, ¼ avocado and 1 tbsp. of cheddar cheese.
- Serve it with lime wedge (optional)

BON APPETITE!

NUTRITION FACTS 1 serving

Calories: 534kcals| Carbohydrates: 57.14g| Protein: 40.3g | Fat: 13.25g | Saturated Fat: 3.12g | Cholesterol: 65.5mg | Sodium: 278mg | Potassium: 1442.7mg | Fiber: 12.75g

HEALTH BENEFITS: Quinoa is high in fiber, which helps in getting rid of CVDs and other metabolic disorders by lowering cholesterol and glucose levels. It has a high capacity to carry oxygen to the brain because it is rich in iron. It also contains riboflavin (Vitamin B2), which keeps brain and muscle cells healthy.

5 DESSERTS

Dessert, the sweet finale to a meal, beckons us into a world of indulgence, pleasure, and culinary artistry. It is the moment where flavors dance on our tongues, captivating our senses and satisfying our cravings. Dessert is a symphony of sweetness, a tantalizing crescendo that elevates a dining experience from mere sustenance to a celebration of decadence.

With each bite, dessert transports us to a realm of pure bliss. It is a realm where chocolate melts on our palate, creamy custards tantalize our taste buds, and fruit bursts with natural sweetness. Dessert is a canvas for creativity, offering an array of textures, colors, and flavors that awaken our senses and ignite our imagination.

More than just a treat for the palate, dessert carries an air of celebration and indulgence. It is a reward for a well-enjoyed meal, a marker of special occasions, and a gesture of hospitality and generosity. Dessert brings people together, fostering connection and creating moments of joy as we share in the delight of each spoonful or forkful.

Dessert is an expression of culinary artistry, where skilled pastry chefs and home bakers alike craft creations that dazzle both the eye and the taste buds. From intricately layered cakes adorned with delicate frosting to artisanal ice creams infused with unique flavors, dessert embodies the creativity and passion of those who bring it to life.

Yet, dessert is more than just a feast for our senses. It embodies a sense of comfort and nostalgia, evoking memories of childhood delights and cherished family recipes passed down through generations. It is a taste of home, a reminder of simpler times, and a source of solace in moments of celebration or introspection.

In the world of dessert, there is something for everyone. From the classic favorites that never fail to satisfy to the bold and innovative creations that push the boundaries of our culinary imagination, dessert invites us to indulge in our desires, to savor the sweetness of life, and to embrace the pleasure that comes with surrendering to temptation.

So, let us relish the enchantment of dessert. Let us delight in the symphony of flavors, the artistry of presentation, and the moments of pure bliss it brings. May we savor each spoonful or forkful, cherishing the joy it ignites within us and the memories it weaves into the tapestry of our lives. In the realm of dessert, let us find a moment of pure indulgence, a celebration of life's sweetness, and a delectable reminder that every meal deserves a grand finale.

Pear And Ginger Crumble:

Serves: 6
Ingredients

- 5 large pears
- ½ cup dried cranberry
- 1/3 cup whole wheat flour
- 2 tsp olive oil
- ½ cup rolled oats
- 2 tbsp shredded coconut

Instructions

- Pre heat the oven up to 375F.
- Peel, quarter and core the pears, then roughly chop and place in a large saucepan. Cover and bring it to boil. Reduce the flame to medium-low and cook for 5 minutes. Stir in cranberries.
- To make the crumble topping, shift the flour and ginger into a bowl. Add the olive oil spread and use your fingertips to rub in until evenly combined. Mix the oats and coconut.
- Sprinkle the topping over the fruit in the dish and bake it for 30 minutes.

Pear And Ginger Crumble

NUTRITION FACTS 1 serving

Calories: 218kcals| Carbohydrates: 48.6g| Protein: 3.7g |
Fat: 1.3g | Saturated
Fat: 0.38g | Cholesterol: 0mg | Sodium: 2.6mg | Potassiu
m: 294mg | Fiber: 8g

HEALTH BENEFITS: Ginger helps in increasing
dopamine and serotonin levels. It has anti-inflammatory
properties that help reduce oxidative stress, inflammation
in joints like in osteoarthritis and lowers bad cholesterol.
It is packed with beneficial plant sterols and stanols.

Buttermilk Pudding:

Serves: 4

Ingredients

- 2 cups butter milk
- 2 cups frozen berries
- 1tbsp. maple syrup
- 1 vanilla bean

Instructions

- Combine the buttermilk in a saucepan. Split the vanilla bean lengthwise, scrape the tiny seeds into the pan and add vanilla bean. Gently heat the mixture until hot but not boiling. Turn off the heat and stand for 10 minutes, then remove the vanilla bean.
- Soak the gelatin in a bowl of cold water for 5 minutes. Squeeze the water and then add gelatin to the buttermilk mixture stir until dissolved.
- Place the berries in a saucepan and gently heat until thawed and juicy. Stir in the maple syrup.
- Pour the buttermilk in the molds and let them cool.

Buttermilk Pudding

NUTRITION FACTS 1 serving

Calories: 85.7kcals| Carbohydrates: 14.9g| Protein: 4.5g | Fat: 1.2g | Saturated Fat: 0.6g | Cholesterol: 5mg | Sodium: 129.7mg | Potassium: 303mg | Fiber: 1.5g

HEALTH BENEFITS: These have a good amount of potassium, folate (vitamin B9), and manganese and are a great source of vitamin C and manganese. The high antioxidant and plant component content of raspberries may be advantageous for heart health and blood sugar regulation and reducing depression.

Chia Coconut Cookies:

Serves: 2

Ingredients

- 4 walnuts
- ½ oz medium dates
- 10g shredded coconut
- ½ tsp. chia seeds
- ½ tsp. vanilla extract
- ½ tsp. cocoa powder

Instructions

- Pre heat oven to 350F. spread walnuts on the baking tray and bake for 4-5 minutes, until lightly toasted. Transfer the walnuts to a plate to cool, then roughly chop.
- Add dates to a food processor and add coconut, cocoa powder, chia seeds, vanilla and 4 walnuts, process until smooth.
- Take a heaped tsp. of chocolate mixture and roll it into a ball. Slightly flatten, then gently press the top into the walnuts. Repeat with the remaining mixture.
- Put the cookies in a single layer in an airtight container, and chill until firm. The cookies can be refrigerated for up to two weeks.

Chia Coconut Cookies

NUTRITION FACTS 1 serving

Calories: 108kcals| Carbohydrates: 8.28g| Protein: 1.88g |
Fat: 8.6g | Saturated
Fat: 3.4g | Cholesterol: 0mg | Sodium: 2.5mg | Potassium:
132.5mg | Fiber: 2.2 g

HEALTH BENEFITS: Chia seeds have a balance of
soluble and insoluble fiber, which act as pre and
probiotics. This means they help feed the beneficial
bacteria in our intestines- the same bacteria that help
produce things like serotonin and other important
neurotransmitters that help regulate your gut brain
connection.

Raspberry and Yogurt Popsicle:

Serves: 8

Ingredients

- 3 large bananas
- 1 cup Greek yogurt
- 7oz frozen raspberries
- 1tsp. vanilla extract

Instructions

- Cut the bananas into 1-inch slices and place in a resealable plastic bag. Expel the excess air, then tightly seal. Freeze for about 6 hours. Until firm.
- Line the sieve with cheesecloth and stand over the bowl, with the bottom of the sieve well clear 0f the base of bowl. Spoon the yogurt into the muslin or cheesecloth, gather up the ends and twist to enclose. Place the saucer on the muslin and weigh down with 400g cans. Place in the fridge to drain for about 4 hours.
- Combine the frozen bananas slices, frozen raspberries, drained yogurt and vanilla in food processor. Process until smooth and evenly combined occasionally stopping and scraping down the side with a rubber spatula.

- Transfer the mixture to an airtight container and freeze it for 6 hours until firm.

BON APPETITE!

NUTRITION FACTS 1 serving

Calories: 93.3kcals| Carbohydrates: 128.7g| Protein: 2g | Fat: 3g | Saturated Fat: 1.7g | Cholesterol: 10.3mg | Sodium: 17.2mg | Potassium: 267mg | Fiber: 2.9g

HEALTH BENEFITS: They have a good amount of potassium, folate (vitamin B9), and manganese and are a great source of vitamin C and manganese. The high antioxidant and plant component content of raspberries may be advantageous for heart health and blood sugar regulation and reducing depression.

Saffron and Pistachio Pudding:

Serves: 4

Ingredients

- ½ cup raw pistachio
- 3 cups unsweetened almond milk
- 1 currant
- 1 pinch saffron
- 1 cinnamon stick
- 2 cardamoms
- 2tbsp. honey
- 1 tsp. semolina

Instructions

- Finely chop or grind half the pistachio. Coarsely chop the other ingredients.
- Combine almond milk, saffron, cinnamon, cardamom in a large saucepan. Allow the mixture to stand for 1 hour if time permits. Bring to a boil, then remove the cinnamon stick and whisk in the honey and semolina.

- Stir the mixture and make it smooth. Stir in finely chopped pistachio and rose water.
- To make syrup boil honey and cardamom in a saucepan. Serve the pudding topped with hot cardamom and honey syrup. (optional)

BON APPETITE!

NUTRITION FACTS 1 serving

Calories: 151kcals| Carbohydrates:13.3 g| Protein: 9.4g | Fat: 7g | Saturated
Fat: 1g | Cholesterol: 3.7mg | Sodium: 95.7mg | Potassiu m: 462.5mg | Fiber: 1.5g

HEALTH BENEFITS: Stress can impair our brain function, saffron is an all-natural mood booster. When you consume saffron, it changes the level of neurotransmitters such as dopamine, nor-epinephrine and serotonin in the brain that helps keep your mood balanced.

ABOUT THE AUTHOR

Hayley Venard, a compassionate advocate for senior well-being, has devoted her entire existence to enriching the lives of our beloved elders. With a remarkable career spanning nursing home administration, consultancy, and the establishment of a non-profit organization dedicated to offering mental health counseling to nursing home residents, Hayley's unwavering commitment knows no bounds. In addition, she owns a home care company, providing essential assistance to seniors in need.

This extraordinary cookbook stands as a testament to Hayley's tireless efforts. It is accompanied by the Brain Bridges Coloring Book and Brain Bridges Puzzle Book, all ingeniously designed to not only ignite joy but also raise crucial funds for mental health services tailored to the unique needs of our cherished seniors. Every page turned, every puzzle solved, and every recipe explored contributes to the noble cause of ensuring mental well-being for those who need it most.

Hayley's compassion knows no limits. She understands that nurturing the minds and spirits of our seniors is a profound duty that calls for unwavering dedication. With these remarkable creations, she aspires to bridge the gaps in mental health services for seniors, providing them with the support, solace, and care they richly deserve.

Let us celebrate Hayley Venard's remarkable journey, her unwavering advocacy, and her noble vision to enhance the lives of our seniors. Together, as we embark on these culinary and creative adventures, we can make a tangible difference in the mental well-being of those who have gifted us with wisdom, love, and a lifetime of memories.

Made in the USA
Columbia, SC
04 July 2023